Coats of Arms

An Introduction to
The Science and Art of Heraldry

Written and Illustrated by
Marc Fountain

Modern History Press

Ann Arbor, MI

ISBN 978-1-61599-695-7 paperback
ISBN 978-1-61599-696-4 hardcover
ISBN 978-1-61599-697-1 eBook

Published by
Modern History Press   www.ModernHistoryPress.com
5145 Pontiac Trail   info@ModernHistoryPress.com
Ann Arbor, MI 48105   Tollfree 888-761-6268 (USA/CAN/PR)

Distributed by Ingram Book Group (USA/CAN/AU)

Library of Congress Cataloging-in-Publication Data

Names: Fountain, Marc, 1965- author, illustrator.
Title: Coats of arms : an introduction to the science and art of heraldry / written and Illustrated by Marc Fountain.
Description: Ann Arbor, MI: Modern History Press, [2022] | Includes bibliographical references and index. | Summary: "Secret codes of knighthood, nobility and royalty are revealed in this full color introductory guide accessible to readers of every age. Discover how to create your own coat of arms and illustrate those of your ancestors. Empowering resource for expressing who you are in art, history, social studies, and genealogy"-- Provided by publisher.
Identifiers: LCCN 2022039325 (print) | LCCN 2022039326 (ebook) | ISBN 9781615996957 (paperback) | ISBN 9781615996964 (hardcover) | ISBN 9781615996971 (epub)
Subjects: LCSH: Heraldry.
Classification: LCC CR21 .F68 2022 (print) | LCC CR21 (ebook) | DDC 929.6--dc23/eng/20220817
LC record available at https://lccn.loc.gov/2022039325
LC ebook record available at https://lccn.loc.gov/2022039326

Contents

Symbols of Identity

For at least sixty thousand years, our ancestors have created symbols. Some of the earliest were made by holding a hand against a rock wall and spraying powdered rock of a contrasting color over the area. The message behind such a symbol might have been, "I was here." Or maybe, "This place belongs to me." Or perhaps, "I belong to this place." Eventually, more symbols appeared, with more messages: "*We* are this family, or this tribe, or this land, or this way of thinking." Symbols painted on walls weren't very portable, though. When members of that family or tribe went far afield, how could they symbolize their identity?

They could paint temporary patterns on their skin.

They could needle permanent patterns into their skin.

They could weave a pattern into fabric, then sew that fabric into clothing.

They could work symbols into jewelry, to be worn openly

    or kept hidden until needed for identification.

They could carve symbols into their weapons or paint symbols onto their shields.

Symbols on weapons tended to be small and intimate, visible mainly to the weapon's owner and (for a few seconds, anyway) to those on the receiving end. A weapon which outlived its first owner sometimes acquired a name of its own. Yet even a weapon as famous as the legendary Excalibur wouldn't be that discernible from other swords during battle.

Shields, on the other hand, provided surfaces large enough to bear symbols recognizable at a distance. At one time or another, warriors in nearly every culture have carried handheld shields into battle. Shield shapes varied depending on the weapons borne by the warriors, and by their opponents.

Aboriginal Australia	Aztec/Mixtec America	Indonesia Polynesia	Warring States China	Sub-Saharan Africa	Ancient Rome

Ancient Egypt	Ancient Greece	Pre-Samurai Japan	Dark Ages Europe	Norman Europe	Heraldic Europe

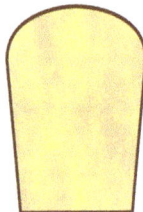

In cultures where the group was more important than the individual, shields were uniform. In Ancient Rome, shields bore symbols of a legion (army) or the whole nation (SPQR, Senatus PopulusQue Romanum, the Senate and People of Rome), delivering one message: civilization and order are coming, whether you wish it or not. To the extent that warriors expressed individuality, it was by spoken names, not symbols.

European Feudalism

In post-Roman Western Europe (after 476 AD), order gave way to chaos. During the ensuing European Dark Ages, repeated attempts were made to restore order. The attempt which succeeded was called feudalism, a re-imagining of the Roman Army structure based upon the holding of land.

A king claimed ownership of all lands within his kingdom's borders. He then assigned fractions of those lands to his generals. The most important fractions were called duchies, and the general responsible was a duke. Borderland fractions were called marches, and the general responsible was a marquis (mar-KEE or MAR-kwis). Inland fractions included counties assigned to counts or viscounts (VY-counts), and baronies assigned to barons. In England, counts are called earls. They rule earldoms.

Although a duke typically held more power and responsibility than a baron, each saw the other as a peer. Each peer was obliged to maintain troops ready to respond at the king's bidding. In the early years of feudalism, peers maintained troops by subdividing their own lands, granting small subholdings to their lieutenants... knights. Peers and knights together were called Gentry. All others were Commoners.

Before 1095, most Europeans stayed close to home. The number of peers being few in any one kingdom, they were all well known to one another (nobilis, hence the words noble and nobility). There was little need to identify themselves by means of consistent symbols. Anyone who bore a shield painted it with whatever pattern he fancied at that moment, and little care was given to avoiding duplication.

The Crusades changed all that. These ultimately futile invasions of someone else's continent produced several lasting consequences, most of them negative for future generations. One of the few positives was that it reminded Western Europe of what civilization looked like. While descendants of the Roman Empire had been killing each other over who would get enough to eat, Muslim astronomers had been naming the stars.

When Europeans tried to unite for battle, they couldn't coordinate. Never mind that they no longer spoke the same language, most couldn't read. Citizens of the Middle East, meanwhile, had been filling university libraries with translations of every text they could find (even texts which contradicted their faith).

Muslim civilization was caught by surprise by the First Crusade, but it regrouped under the leadership of a Kurdish general who commanded forces from Syria through Egypt. Saladin crushed the Second Crusade, yet was so courteous in victory that he forced Europeans to reconsider what it meant to be noble. "Might *is* right" was replaced by "Might *for* right." Sound familiar? Europeans couldn't bring themselves to acknowledge Saladin as their role model. Instead, they resurrected myths of Celtic leader Artorius, rebranded him as Arthur, and used this imaginary king and his knights to espouse ideals of chivalry.

At the same time, Europe standardized battlefield identification based on shield decoration. Each king began to consistently bear his own unique symbols on his shield. Each peer did likewise with his own unique symbols, as did each knight. This satisfied two needs: knowledge at a glance as to which of one's allies were where during battle, and opportunity for self-aggrandizement. Another lesson learned from fighting in deserts was the adoption of surcoats to keep hot sunshine away from metal armor. These fabrics too became surfaces for the display of the same symbols, hence the term *coat* of arms.

England	Scotland	Waleton	Samlesbury	Praers	Worthington	Galicia	France

Heraldry is the art and profession of creating designs within shield-shaped outlines meant to identify important individuals and their descendants, as well as organizations (towns, schools, corporations) and nations. These designs often come surrounded by additional symbols such as helms, crowns or crests. Although few of us bear actual shields in the modern world, many today print their ancestors' armorial symbols onto paper, engrave them into jewelry or tableware, and carve them into wood and stone.

Chevalier, Caballero, Cavalry Officer, Knight

As medieval European warriors added articulated steel plates to their chain mail armor, these increasingly lobster-like suits evolved along two traditions: wartime battlefield and peacetime jousting.

The vision of a "knight in shining armor" comes from the peacetime jousting tradition, in which two men and their horses performed carefully staged head-on collisions then paused to judge who had taken the greater hurt. Jousting armor, constructed of heavy gauge steel, favored impenetrability over agility and stamina. As a result, a knight knocked to the ground during a joust, even if uninjured, struggled to regain his footing. Mounting his horse again was usually out of the question. That required the assistance of esquires... and sometimes a winch.

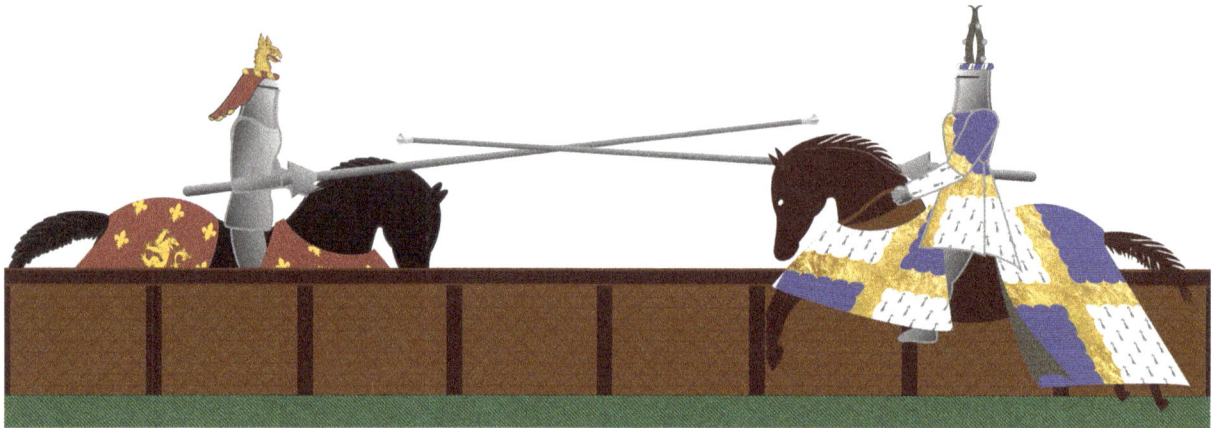

In sharp contrast, army battles might rage for hours, and a priority for every participant was to *avoid* taking direct impacts. Battlefield armor, constructed with steel thickness minimized where possible to lighten the load on the wearer, favored agility and stamina. A knight wearing medieval battlefield armor, when unhorsed, was every bit as nimble and lethal as a present-day Marine, perfectly able to chase down the foot soldier who unhorsed him.

Flags Versus Heraldry

Flag and shield decoration both began with the same purpose: advertisement on the battlefield. Because the knight bearing the decorated shield was elevated on horseback as a cavalry officer, he naturally bore his personal colors high enough to be seen by the foot soldiers under his command. But an infantry officer marching alongside his soldiers needed some other way of elevating the colors to be rallied round, and flags were the solution. Why would knights abandon their horses and walk on level with commoners? Because advertising during battle can attract the wrong sort of attention. Besides, knights could show off their equestrian skills during peacetime.

Jousting favored pageantry. Horses and knights were decorated as vividly as today's race cars and drivers, while heralds (tournament organizers) had authority to regulate those decorations. Should two knights arrive wearing the same symbols and colors, heralds would insist that one or both make changes sufficient to differentiate between them. The changed symbols were then officially recorded, and would be expected at future tournaments. As the decades passed, sons inherited their fathers' symbols and colors. Heraldry thus came to identify the male lines of important families, and illustrate alliances / marriages between them. This soon produced heraldic designs too complex to be interpreted except at close range.

Battlefields favored efficiency. As firearms became ever better at piercing armor plating, attracting attention became a liability. Wise leaders started dressing more quietly, assigning the task of rallying troops to a foot soldier carrying a flag on a pole. This is why flag designs have tended to remain simple down through the centuries: because clear identification at a distance continues to be their priority.

Ruling families and the lands they rule typically have coats of arms *and* flags. Usually, they differ:

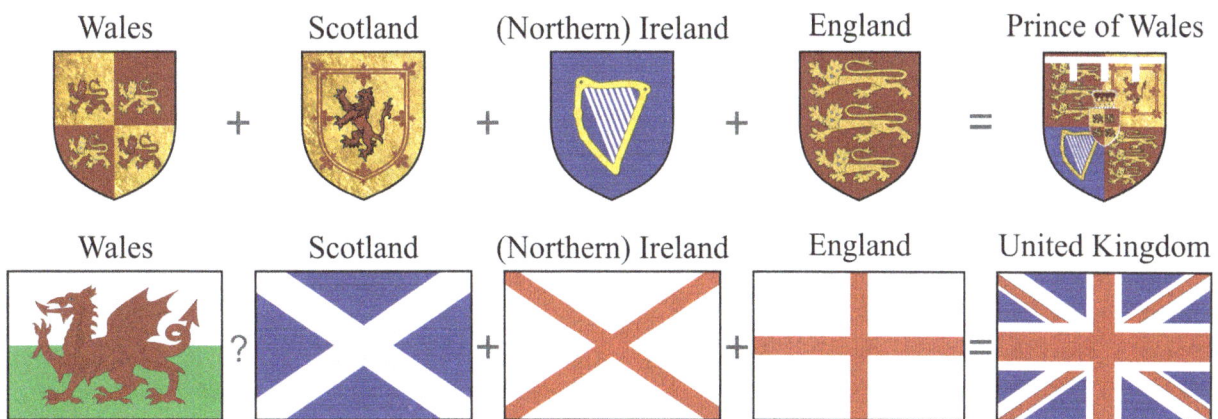

Wales	Scotland	(Northern) Ireland	England	Prince of Wales

Wales	Scotland	(Northern) Ireland	England	United Kingdom

Of course, there are exceptions:

Arms of Baron Baltimore	Flag of the State of Maryland	Arms of George Washington	Flag of the City of Washington, DC	Arms of the Kingdom of Hawai'i	Flag of the State of Hawaii

Shield Shapes

By the 1400s, handheld shields were becoming obsolete on the battlefield. Within a further century, jousting had likewise faded into history, but the tradition of displaying heraldic symbols on shield-shaped surfaces had been firmly ingrained in European culture. Freed from the need to stay true to practical shield shapes, heraldic artists began wrapping armorial symbols in all kinds of outlines:

Women in most cultures did not carry shields. In Europe, whenever women needed to bear the family's arms, they were expected to use a non-shield-shaped outline. The lozenge (diamond) was the preferred shape, with the tall oval a non-military alternative for any gender. In recent years, especially in nations without rigidly enforced heraldry, women often use shield shapes, as is their equal right.

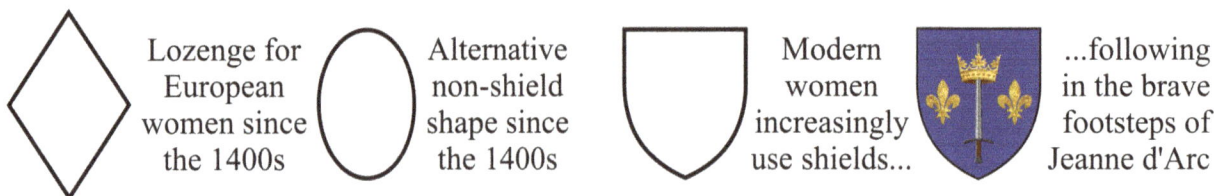

Lozenge for European women since the 1400s

Alternative non-shield shape since the 1400s

Modern women increasingly use shields...

...following in the brave footsteps of Jeanne d'Arc

Europe's armorial tradition is just one of several worldwide. The system of circular *mon* symbols among Japanese families and companies, in particular, is every bit as extensive as heraldry. Other nations around the world have adapted aspects of European heraldry to fit their needs, using shield shapes and foreground symbols (charges) from their own cultures, frequently to stunning effect. That's the art of heraldry: to be in harmony with a recognized standard, and yet to express individuality.

Japan   Botswana   Lesotho   South Sudan

Trademarks Versus Heraldry

In the U.S., a part of government named the Patent and Trademark Office registers legal ownership of names and symbols used by corporations and other organizations. Most countries around the world have such an office. Countries such as England and Scotland, though, have an additional part of government tasked with maintaining control over heraldic symbols used within that country. To be armigerous (ar-MIJ-er-us), that is to legally bear a coat of arms there, it is necessary to petition that country's College of Arms for a grant of that coat.

The United States does not have a College of Arms, so individuals and families and organizations are free to use any heraldic symbols they wish as long as the symbols do not duplicate existing trademarks. But why use someone else's symbol when there are so many unique combinations as yet unclaimed?

The reason why the United States doesn't have a College of Arms is that the Thirteen Colonies fought to disentangle themselves from German kings and English nobility in the 1700s. Perhaps to no great surprise, UnitedStatesians have spent the subsequent centuries regretting what our forebears cast away. It's no accident that the theme song chosen for *The Lone Ranger* was the *William Tell Overture*. Our idealization of cowboys is our substitute for tales of archers and swordsmen. And, at least as of this printing, more US girls have grown up to marry princes than to become Supreme Court justices.

Contrast

The original goal of a coat of arms was the same as that of a road sign: fast comprehension at a distance. Light symbols on a dark background, and dark symbols on a light background (strong contrast), are easy to read. Dark on dark, and light on light (poor contrast), are difficult to read. Modern equipment can distinguish between millions of hues and shades, but a limited, stark palette is easier for humans to read.

Strong Contrast - Easy to Read

TINCTURE BEHIND METAL	METAL BEHIND TINCTURE	FUR BEHIND TINCTURE
TINCTURE BEHIND METAL	METAL BEHIND TINCTURE	FUR BEHIND TINCTURE
TINCTURE BEHIND METAL		

Poor Contrast - Difficult to Read

TINCTURE BEHIND TINCTURE	METAL BEHIND METAL	FUR BEHIND METAL
TINCTURE BEHIND TINCTURE	METAL BEHIND METAL	FUR BEHIND FUR
TINCTURE BEHIND TINCTURE		

Colors–Tinctures and Metals and Furs

Black and red and blue have always been the dominant *dark* colors in heraldry. Dark green and dark purple do occur as well, but never as often as dark blue and dark red. This is partly due to the limitations of tinctures (dyes and paints and inks) available nine hundred years ago: attempts at green or purple could end up appearing bluish or reddish on the final product, especially as the material faded over time. Safer then to stick with the primary colors. Politics played a part, too: the kings of England favored dark red in their own arms, while the kings of France favored dark blue in theirs, so nobles and knights tended to follow the lead of their sovereigns rather than risk colors which might call their loyalty into question.

Gold and silver have always been the dominant *light* colors in heraldry since polished metals don't have to be painted, although yellow paint or ink is often used in place of gold, and white in place of silver.

Furs, the third category of colors after tinctures and metals, arose from European nobles' fondness for items of clothing made from conjoined pelts of ermine and various other animals. A furry shield not being particularly practical, stylized patterns were painted on shields in mimicry of fur.

Some people since the 1800s have tried to assign meaning (hope, courage, loyalty, etc.) to various colors. This is nonsense. The only meaning in a green coat of arms is the original bearer saying, "I like the color green," or possibly, "My family name is Green." Puns abound in heraldry: the family name of the mother of Queen Elizabeth II was Bowes-Lyon, hence a coat of arms depicting archers' bows and lions.

Colors–Hatching

Coats of arms aren't always illustrated in full color. They may be engraved into stone or silverware, carved into wood, embossed in gold leaf onto leather book covers, or printed on paper using just one color of ink. How then can the artist indicate multiple colors? Centuries ago, a standard set of lines and dots was established: vertical lines for red, horizontal lines for blue, dots for gold, no dots or lines at all for silver, and so forth. Now that you know what you're looking for, you'll find hatching in the most interesting places.

Tinctures	Metals	Furs
Sable (Black) 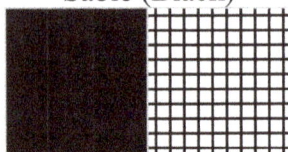	**Argent (Silver / White)** 	**Ermine** 
Gules (Red) 	**Or (Gold / Yellow)** 	**Vair** 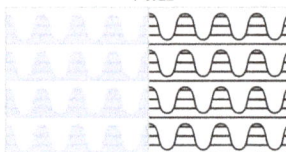
Azure (Blue) 		

And now you know what the shield on the eagle on a US $1 bill looks like in full color...

Vert (Green)

Purpure (Purple)

Other hues and shades are avoided because they are too easily confused with the nearest standard color or with stains of battle, and battlefield confusion tends to be fatal. A very few nonstandard colors have found uses even though they depart from the tradition of dark tinctures, light metals and light furs. Cendrée is ideal for steel helms, blades, etc. Brunâtre serves equally well for wooden objects and bears. But keep Céleste away from Argent and Vair. Remember, a coat's goal is easy recognition at a glance.

Céleste (Pale Blue)	Cendrée (Cinders / Steel)	Brunâtre (Brown Fur)
		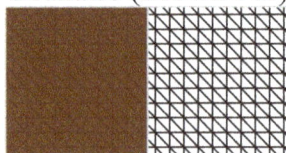

Within the Shield

The art of heraldry came from decorating physical shields: painting the field (flat background surface), then optionally affixing charges (flat foreground figures) on that surface. As a result, heraldry does not try to suggest depth like a photograph or a perspective drawing. Instead, heraldic depth is more akin to collages of construction paper: a stack of flat layers. When in doubt, reach for scissors and glue rather than a paintbrush.

A coat of arms can consist of just a field layer (solid color or a division pattern)

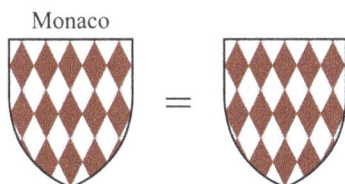

Monaco

or a field layer with a charge (figure) in front

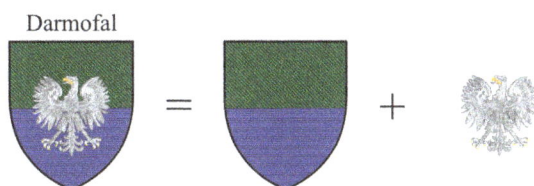

Darmofal

or a field layer with an Ordinary (a category of large geometric charge) in front.

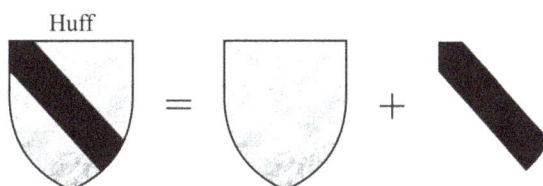

Huff

Ordinaries and other charges can reside on the same layer.

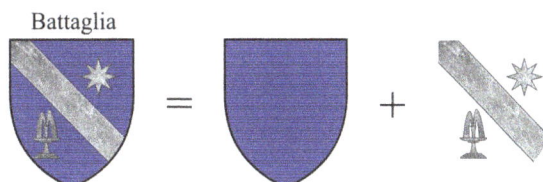

Battaglia

Charges can be placed in front of an Ordinary.

Hamblett

And, within reason, layers can carry on being stacked.

Tempest

Divisions

The simplest coats have a field layer only. The field can be all one color:

or the field can be parted into divisions. Several of the more popular party fields are:

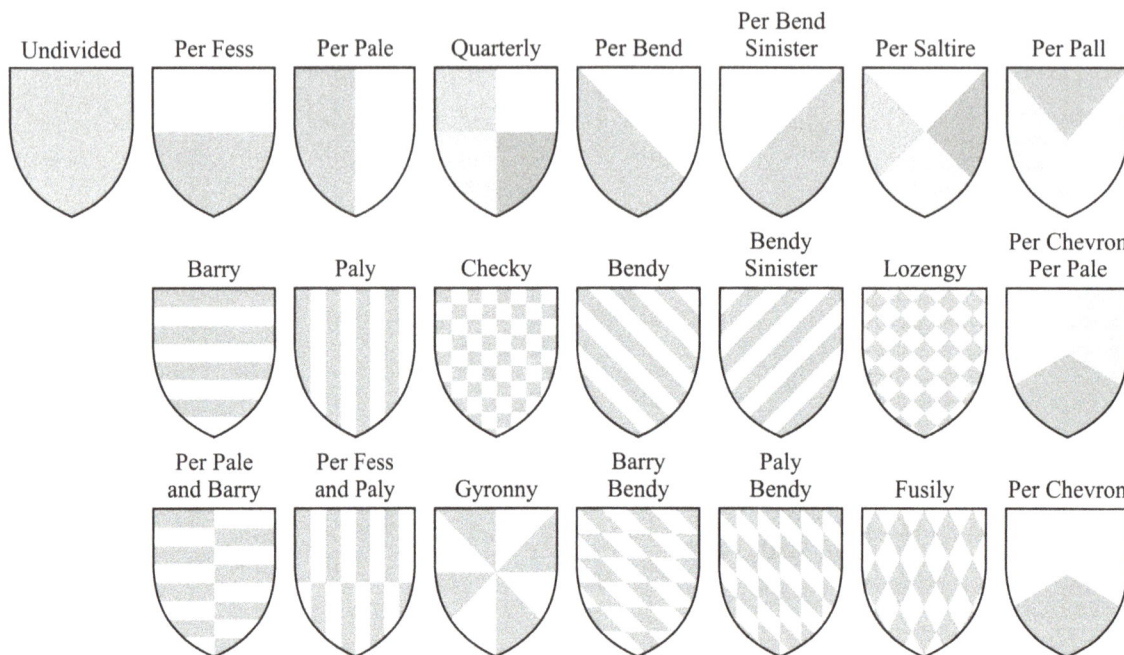

Undivided	Per Fess	Per Pale	Quarterly	Per Bend	Per Bend Sinister	Per Saltire	Per Pall

Barry	Paly	Checky	Bendy	Bendy Sinister	Lozengy	Per Chevron Per Pale

Per Pale and Barry	Per Fess and Paly	Gyronny	Barry Bendy	Paly Bendy	Fusily	Per Chevron

The word Sinister is simply the Latin word for left (the Latin word for right being Dexter). Important: this is left and right from the *bearer's* point of view behind the shield. From *our* point of view as we look at a coat of arms, we see Dexter to our left and Sinister to our right. Same as theatre: stage right is audience left.

Each division can receive any color because they are all on the same layer, neither in front of nor behind each other. Metal can rest comfortably alongside metal, fur alongside fur, or tincture alongside tincture. Complex divisions do have a weakness, though: additional objects placed in front of them may struggle for legibility against a too-busy background (McWilliams, Barber).

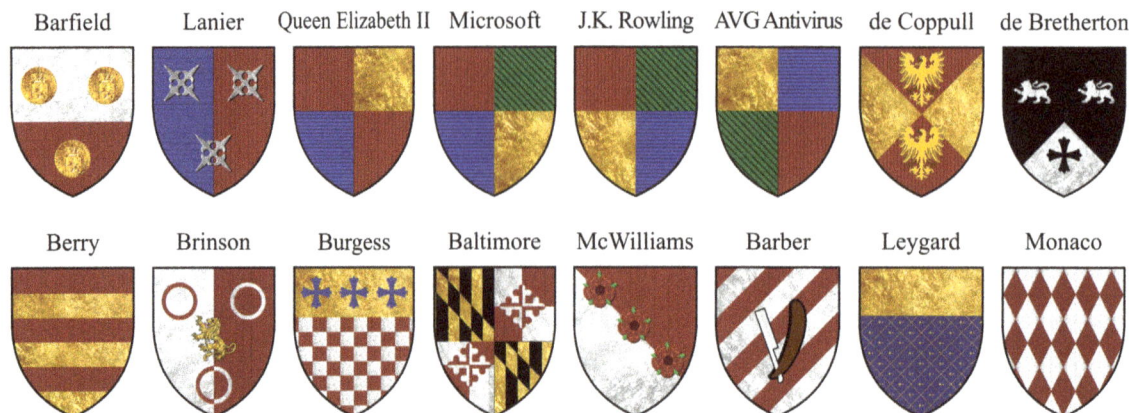

Barfield	Lanier	Queen Elizabeth II	Microsoft	J.K. Rowling	AVG Antivirus	de Coppull	de Bretherton

Berry	Brinson	Burgess	Baltimore	McWilliams	Barber	Leygard	Monaco

Ordinaries–Large Geometric Shapes

It is when foreground layers are added that the need for high contrast comes into play.

The shapes called Ordinaries, Diminutives and Sub-Ordinaries were inspired by the physical construction of a shield. Rather than one smooth sheet of material, a pre-heraldic shield was usually built up in layers with strapped reinforcements. Depending on the maker's choices, these straps might be visible on the front face of the shield. The handicraft of applying metal straps over a background layer was a precursor to the art of heraldry. In this next set of illustrations, black is the background field layer and white is the foreground layer. In 3D renderings of such shields, you would be able to feel the foreground layer as a smooth raised surface.

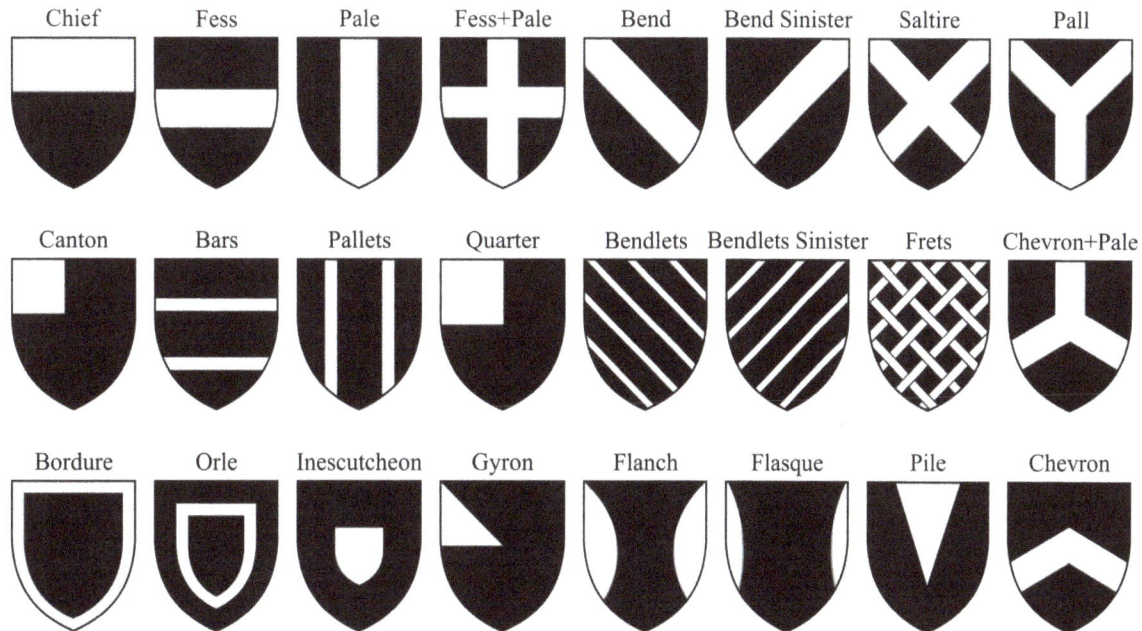

Chief	Fess	Pale	Fess+Pale	Bend	Bend Sinister	Saltire	Pall

Canton	Bars	Pallets	Quarter	Bendlets	Bendlets Sinister	Frets	Chevron+Pale

Bordure	Orle	Inescutcheon	Gyron	Flanch	Flasque	Pile	Chevron

Note the distinction: Barry, Paly and Bendy (Divisions, previous page) cause one edge of a single layer to be a different color from its opposite edge. Bars, Pallets and Bendlets (Ordinaries) are foreground objects which leave the background layer visible at both edges. Bordure leaves the *middle* of the background visible. An Ordinary in front of a field can form the whole of a coat of arms (Webb, Schulz). An Ordinary can share the same layer with other charges (van Schrieck, Holliman, Clayton-Le-Moors, Garrett, Parker). An Ordinary can be charged with charges (Drewry, Hill, Hamblett, Coker, Twine, Sharp, Hull). Ordinaries can overlie other Ordinaries (de Halsall, Hull) which in turn may be charged with charges (Tempest).

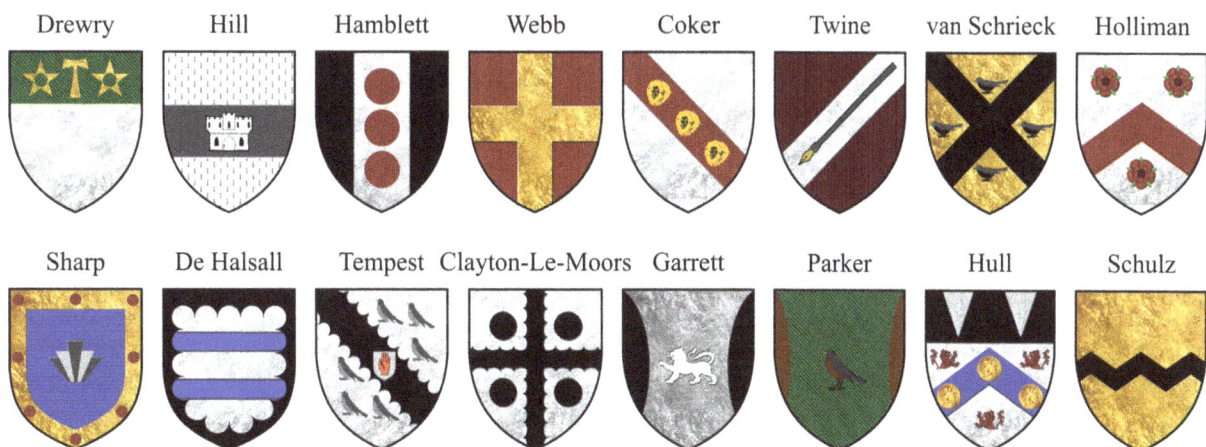

Drewry	Hill	Hamblett	Webb	Coker	Twine	van Schrieck	Holliman

Sharp	De Halsall	Tempest	Clayton-Le-Moors	Garrett	Parker	Hull	Schulz

Edges

Although straight edges are by far the most popular way to separate divisions of a party shield, certain repeating patterns of curves or angles have also been used, many since heraldry's early days.

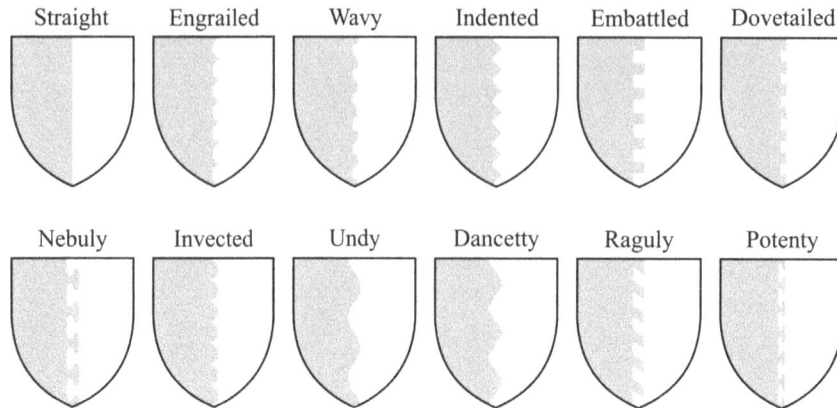

Straight	Engrailed	Wavy	Indented	Embattled	Dovetailed

Nebuly	Invected	Undy	Dancetty	Raguly	Potenty

Note: edges are not lines. Look closely at the examples above. One part of the division gives way to its neighbor without having a third-colored line object in between. When rendered in stained glass, the lead between sections of glass is unavoidably visible, but the lead is not a component of the design. Artists often mistakenly depict divided shields as if they were paned windows. This is incorrect. Don't emphasize edges.

The distinction between Wavy and Undy is frequency: undulations are gentle, long waves. Similarly, Dancetty is Indented with fewer and more pronounced teeth, while Raguly is Embattled at an angle.

Engrailed and Invected need extra clarification. They are the same pattern, just mirror image. The distinction is which way the points are pointed: outbound is Engrailed; inbound is Invected. But outbound or inbound from what? When one surface is divided into parts, Dexter and upper are superior to Sinister and lower, so Per Pale Engrailed means the points stick out toward the right. Per Pale Invected, toward the left.

The distinction is clearer when edges define a foreground figure resting in front of the field. A Pale Engrailed has points sticking outward from both its sides; a Pale Invected, inbound. The other edge patterns can either be mirrors of one another (as in Wavy and Indented below) or not (as in Undy and Dancetty).

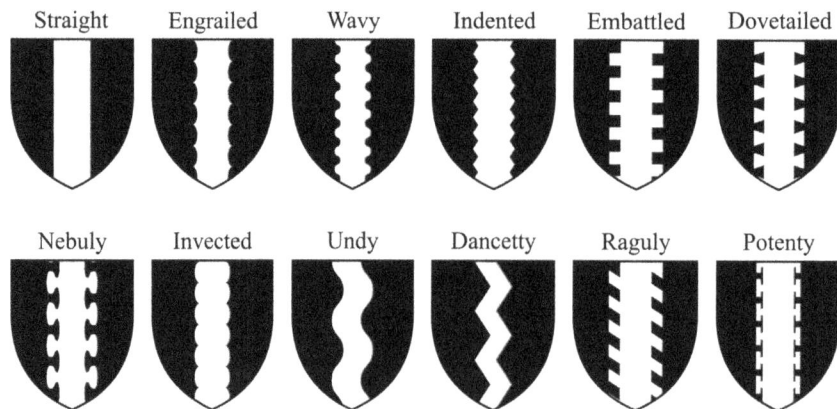

Straight	Engrailed	Wavy	Indented	Embattled	Dovetailed

Nebuly	Invected	Undy	Dancetty	Raguly	Potenty

Charges

Simple geometric figures with strong silhouettes are fine up to a point, but there are thousands of other symbols available. The following pages show just a few of the possibilities. These symbols, called charges, are layered in front of the field, or in front of Ordinaries. When selecting charges, keep strong contrast in mind: a brown hawk is lost in front of a black background.

Charges–Weapons & Tools

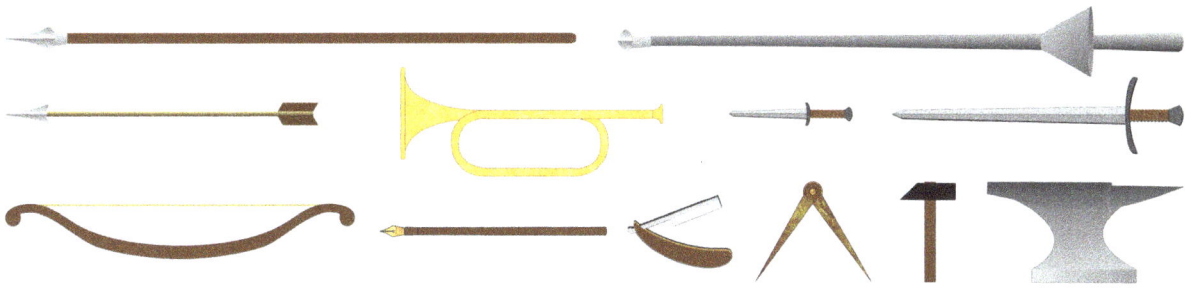

Understandably, depictions of weapons are popular charges, as are the tools of other trades.

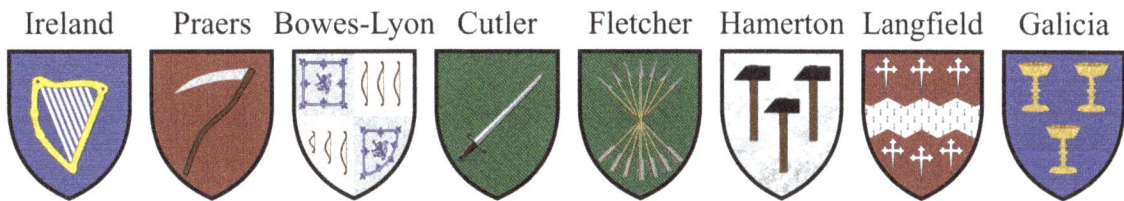

Ireland Praers Bowes-Lyon Cutler Fletcher Hamerton Langfield Galicia

Charges–Suns, Stars, Moons, Planets

Nine centuries years ago, the inventors of heraldry didn't know that the sun is a star, so they categorized symbols meant to represent the sun separately from those meant to represent nighttime stars. In modern usage, the distinction is apparent size. Because our sun is hundreds of thousands of times closer to us than the other stars, we can see it as a disk rather than just a point of light. The disk can be partially hidden by the horizon at sunrise and sunset, or by intervening clouds (when it's called a sunburst). Also, our sun is usually depicted as gold, while other celestial objects may be any heraldic color, or proper (true to life) colors.

When seen from above our atmosphere, stars do not twinkle. But because our ancestors saw nighttime stars from ground level, the intervening air gave them the impression that stars have points. Many coats of arms, and a fair number of national flags, bear depictions of stars and other pointy objects.

Ovéquiz Washington Lai Tepes Vaden Moore Sprinkle Kowalczyk

Charges–Plants

Scotland	Ireland	England	France	Canada	Rome

Some plants have taken on national symbolism, while others are chosen for personal meaning.

Holliman	Sandbach	Dymek	Samlesbury	Cole	Cerrato	Montgomery	Nibbs

Charges–Animals

Animals both real and mythical from all over the planet have been used as charges in coats of arms.

England	Bevan	Blackwell	Westward	Waleton	Day	Columbers	Godfrey

Charges–Small Geometric Shapes

In addition to the Ordinaries, some of the most ancient and often encountered geometric charges are:

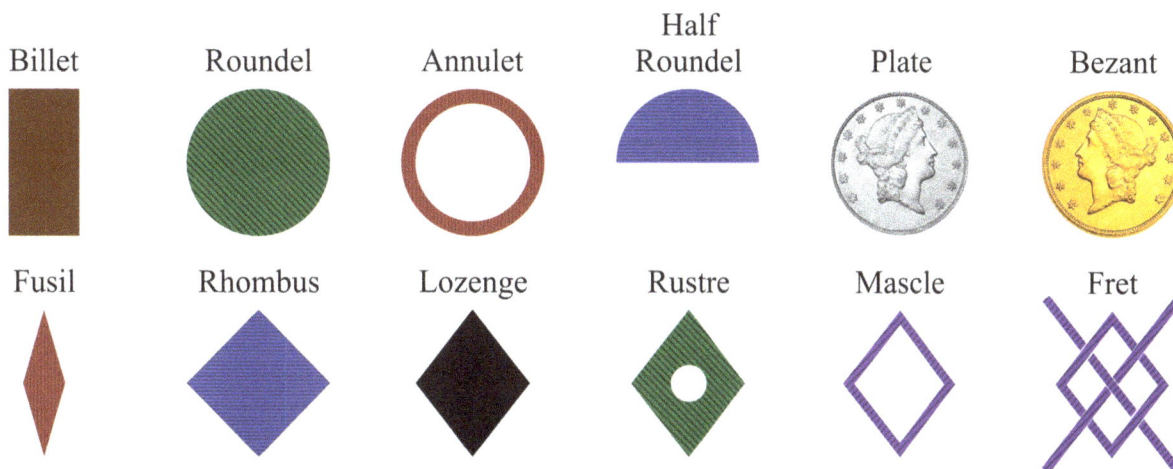

Billet Roundel Annulet Half Roundel Plate Bezant

Fusil Rhombus Lozenge Rustre Mascle Fret

Geometric charges can occur as single objects or in sets of two or more. They can be placed in front of an Ordinary (Hamblett). They can suggest an Ordinary which isn't there (Marshall, Cornwall).

Marshall Hamblett Leygard Cherry Hull Steele Cornwall Cranford

Charges–Letters & Symbols

The Romans emblazoned the letters SPQR (Senate and People of Rome) on all manner of objects. In heraldry, though, the use of Roman letters *as* charges on coats of arms is not encouraged (especially not someone's initials). Still, occasional exceptions occur, such as on the town arms of Seclin in France. Letters from other alphabets fall under the same logic. Three Greek or Cyrillic letters are no more acceptable *as* charges on the field than are three Roman letters. Shields are not the place for acronyms. The same admonition applies against numerals. They are not proper heraldic charges by themselves.

Letters and numbers *on* a charge, however (for example, on the pages of an open book), are quite acceptable, and are a perennial favorite on coats of arms of universities and libraries, because the *book* is the symbol, and it is the nature of a book to have letters and numbers printed on its pages.

Scientific symbols and their more arcane ancestors (alchemical and astrological) have a bit more leeway because they are representations of concepts not sounds. Rule of thumb: if it makes the onlooker try to read it ($E = mc^2$) or sound it out, it shouldn't be used *as* a charge directly on the field of a shield.

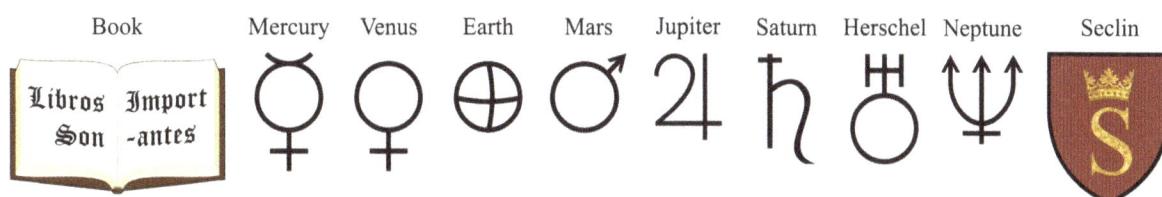

Book Mercury Venus Earth Mars Jupiter Saturn Herschel Neptune Seclin

Libros Import Son -antes

Initials, Ciphers, Monograms

Although letters from the Roman alphabet are discouraged on coats of arms, they take center stage in a separate form of identification: initials and ciphers and monograms inspired by the user's name. An initial is the first letter in a word. Several initials together are called an acronym, but that's not important right now. A cipher is two or more letters combined yet separable. If you remove one letter from a cipher, the remaining letters will still be intact. A monogram is two or more letters merged into a single symbol. If you remove one letter from a monogram, the remaining letters will be damaged.

Nicholas Godfrey	Tom Twine	Michelle Burke	Xenoveva Ovéquiz	James Fox Meadow	Catarina Fuentes	Elizabete Fuentes	Elizabeth II Regina

These figures may be drafted to exacting detail, much like a company logo. Or they may be written freehand, much like a signature but using fewer letters. Simpler to create than coats of arms, they can also be used in heraldic countries without seeking permission from a College of Arms. In countries without a monarch, letters are encountered far more frequently than coats of arms on personal stationery, tableware, etc. When only one letter is engraved (typically the initial of a family surname), it has somewhat the utility of a coat of arms, identifying the male line of the family on items inherited from generation to generation. Items bearing ciphers and monograms, however, while certainly inheritable, refer only to the original owner.

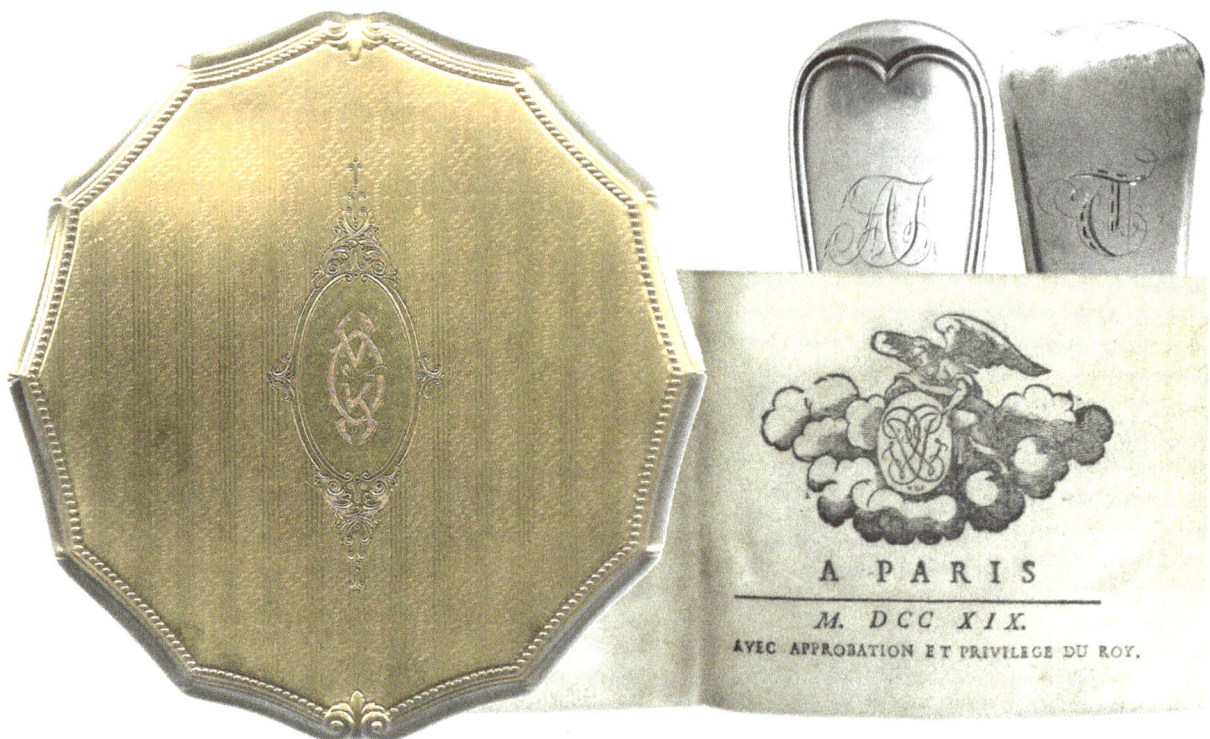

Beyond the Shield

In most cases, the symbols within a shield do not identify the bearer's social rank. Being entitled literally means being granted a title—royal or noble or chivalric—to be indicated outside the shield.

Crest

Torse or circlet

Helm

Mantling

Supporters

Compartment

Entitlement as Obligation

Knighthood was originally both a reward for past military service and an obligation to render future service if summoned. This held particularly true when the grant of knighthood was accompanied by a grant of land. In early centuries, a noble created his own knights and granted them subsets of his own land. Today, only monarchs create knights, and modern knighthoods are seldom granted with land.

Effectively all knights today are created as members of one or another knightly order. In the UK, the Order of the Garter is the highest and rarest form the monarch can grant. The Order of the British Empire is the most populous. Knighthood today is granted for civilian service as well as military service, which occasionally leads to discord. Several military recipients objected when Queen Elizabeth II granted the lowest level of O.B.E. to The Beatles for their civilian service as musical ambassadors.

Knighthood is not hereditary. A land grant might be inherited by a knight's heir, as would any coat of arms granted to that knight, but the title of knight would not be inherited. On occasion, monarchs grant a higher rank of knighthood, the hereditary title Baronet. Despite the confusingly similar names, Baronet is the highest chivalric (knightly) title, quite distinct from Baron, the lowest noble (peer) title.

To recognize the sort of service which saves a nation, and to originally assemble that nation by merging fiefdoms into a kingdom, the notion of hereditary nobility was invented. If the US had formed as a feudal kingdom, a king would rule from Washington, DC, and a noble would rule each state.

As monarchies such as the UK transitioned from feudalism to constitutional government, noble families continued to inherit seats in the House of Lords (equivalent to the US Senate) while untitled citizens began to elect untitled Members of Parliament (MPs) to sit in the House of Commons (equivalent to the US House of Representatives). During the century after World War One, the nobility's influence on UK government was steadily eroded. Many noble families survive, yet few retain their ancestral land holdings and fewer still have a voice in government, which is unfortunate. Heredity provides a long perspective rarely found in republics.

Helms

The helm or helmet is as strongly related to the image of a European warrior as his sword and shield. As medieval battlefield and jousting traditions gradually gave way to modern forms of combat, the heraldic helmet survived only in art, standardized as an indication of the bearer's social rank.

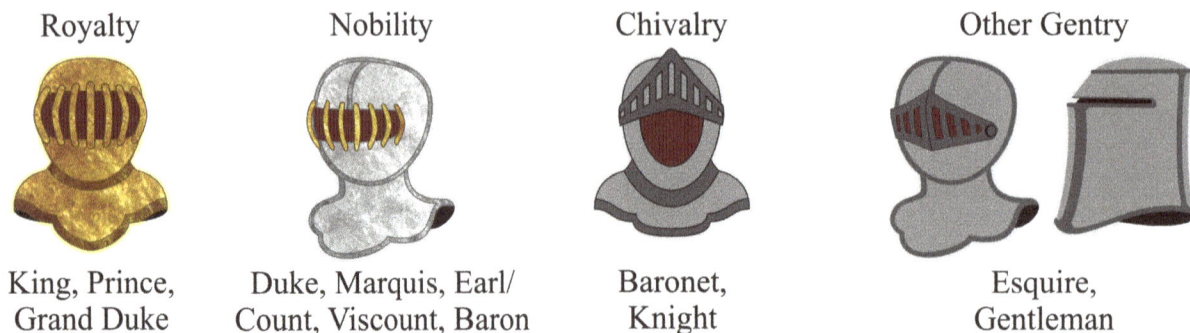

Royalty	Nobility	Chivalry	Other Gentry
King, Prince, Grand Duke	Duke, Marquis, Earl/ Count, Viscount, Baron	Baronet, Knight	Esquire, Gentleman

Royal families (Kings/Queens, Princes/Princesses, ruling Grand Dukes/Duchesses) use a gold helm facing forward, with permanently mounted gold eye protection.

Noble families (Dukes, Marquises, Earls/Counts, Viscounts, Barons) use a silver helm facing to one side, with permanently mounted gold eye protection.

Chivalric persons (Baronets, Knights) use a steel helm facing forward, with moveable visor raised (fun fact: today's military salute came from the motion of a European knight's hand to raise the visor).

Other Gentry (Esquires, Gentlemen) use a steel helm facing to one side, with moveable visor closed or with no visor at all (a jousting helm of heavy steel with only a slit to see through).

Women in Europe traditionally did not display helms above their coats unless they were ruling queens. In the age of women surgeons and fighter pilots, however, there's no excuse to deny them a helm if they wish it, especially in countries such as the US where government does not regulate heraldry.

The tradition which should be adhered to, though, is rank. Anyone wishing to bear a coat of arms may use either helm for Other Gentry. If one of your ancestors was a knight or a noble or a royal, it is reasonable to depict that *ancestor*'s coat of arms with headgear correct for that ancestor's rank and culture. But unless you yourself are a knight or a noble or a royal, onlookers will find it presumptuous that your *own* coat of arms bears the headgear of a rank to which you are not entitled.

Indicating rank by metal hat shape is mainly a European convention, but every society makes class distinctions (warrior/chieftain/monarch) (employee/manager/shareholder) (student/teacher/principal).

Indigenous American empires including the Aztec and Maya had particularly well established class structures. Despite centuries of European conquest and repeated attempts to erase original cultures, many indigenous noble families sustained their lineage, passing their own titles down the generations alongside immigrant Spanish and Portuguese noble families, often adopting European-style coats of arms yet using symbols from their own cultures for charges and helms and crests. Other First Nations citizens value tribal identity over family or personal identity, much like the Highlanders of Scotland.

Royal Crowns and Noble Coronets

Crowns are the insignia of royalty. Coronets are the insignia of nobility. The distinction, with few exceptions, is that a crown has one or more arches which reach all the way over the top of the wearer's head. Coronets may have projections rising from the rim, but these projections do not meet as arches.

In real life, wearing a heavy metal hat without padding is uncomfortable. During ceremonies, crowns and coronets are worn over fabric caps, most often dark red velvet edged with a headband of ermine fur. In heraldry, crowns and coronets can be depicted with or without the cap. Important: both parts of the cap (velvet and ermine) appear, or neither do. They are not separable.

Ruling Grand Duke of Luxembourg — Ruling Prince of Monaco — King or Ruling Queen of England — Grafen von Zinzendorf und Pottendorf

A royal crown can be worn on the royal helm, or the crown can appear without the helm, resting on the top edge of the shield or in the air above it, often oversized. Likewise, a noble coronet can be worn on the noble helm, or the coronet can appear without the helm, resting on the top edge of the shield or in the air above it, often oversized, with or without the cap. Additionally, because a noble's coronet has no arches, the absence of the cap allows room for the noble crest to rise up from within. Crowns and coronets may be drawn level or tilted slightly back as seems appropriate. Appropriateness is set in each monarchy by that nation's College of Arms. Some of the hundreds of variations include:

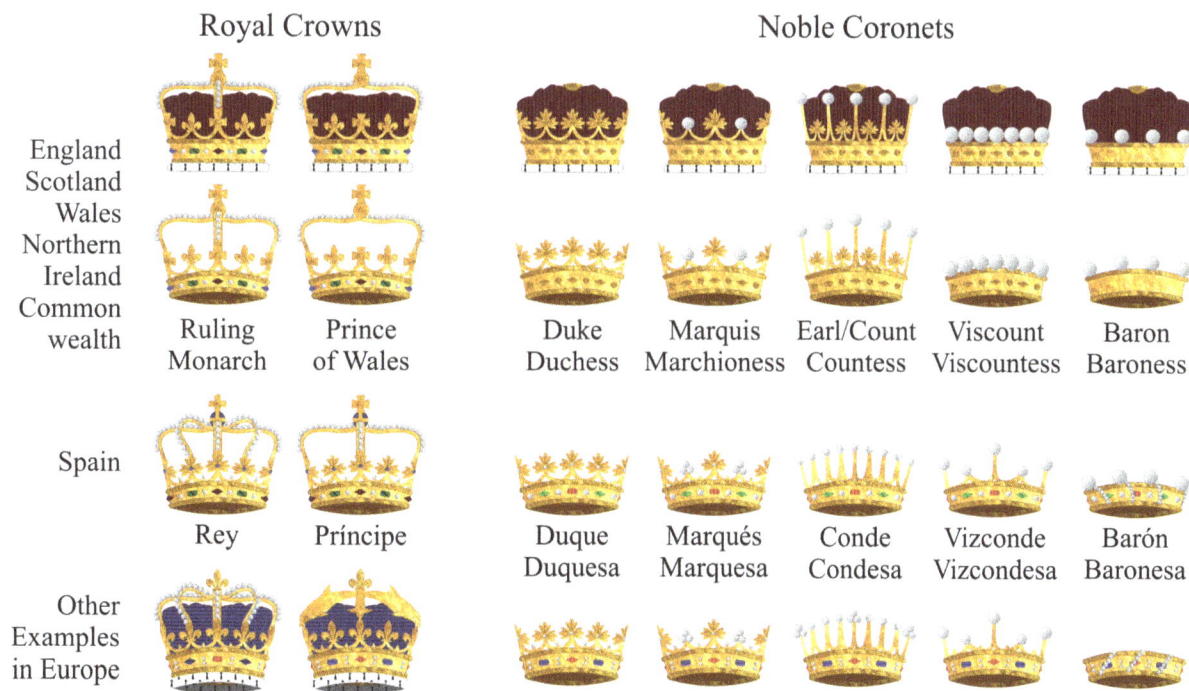

	Royal Crowns		Noble Coronets				
England Scotland Wales Northern Ireland Common wealth	Ruling Monarch	Prince of Wales	Duke Duchess	Marquis Marchioness	Earl/Count Countess	Viscount Viscountess	Baron Baroness
Spain	Rey	Príncipe	Duque Duquesa	Marqués Marquesa	Conde Condesa	Vizconde Vizcondesa	Barón Baronesa
Other Examples in Europe							

Circlets, Torses, Crest Coronets, Mural Coronets

Circlets are headbands of metal which disguise whatever connections are required to anchor a crest device to the top of a helm. They can also hide anchor points for mantling. Even though circlets are sometimes drawn with suggestions of embedded jewels, circlets are always just one color (usually gold).

Torses are headbands of twisted fabric which serve the same function. The six visible folds of a torse alternate between the primary metal and tincture of the coat of arms, with metal always leftmost.

A crest coronet is a torse of a different color. While popular in ancient achievements, often with a crest device rising through the center, it gives the impression that the wearer presumes to noble rank. As a result, its use in modern arms is strongly discouraged. An armiger rightly entitled to wear a coronet would wear a noble's *silver* helm. Armigers entitled only to wear steel helms should not wear coronets.

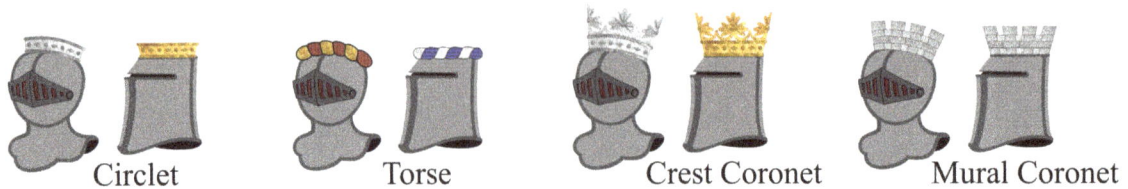

Circlet   Torse   Crest Coronet   Mural Coronet

A mural coronet is another historical anachronism. It often encircles the crest above the civic arms of a town or city. Sometimes it was granted to army generals in recognition of a victory or a long career of exemplary service to king and country. In all other circumstances, its use on a helm is best avoided.

Crests

Crests atop a helm originally had a practical purpose: to ward off blows to the top of the head. Firefighters today still wear hard hats with a crest ridge to deflect falling debris.

Crests evolved from practicality to pageantry via jousting. Much as ships and automobiles once bore figural mascots on their prows, participants in jousts wore symbols on top of their helms. The symbol chosen for the crest could be a charge from the coat of arms, or a separate symbol such as animal horns, or an upraised arm holding a sword, or the head or upper half of an animal (possibly also holding a sword). When a disembodied head or arm is depicted, it is termed Erased (e.g., dragon's head erased).

As something of a shorthand, armigerous families often use the crest and torse alone instead of the full achievement of arms on small items such as table silver, stationery and signet rings. This has led to the frequent but wrong use of the phrase "family crest" to mean anything heraldic.

An armigerous family is identified by its coat of arms (the symbols within the shield outline). The crest alone is not unique enough (nor officially recorded as unique enough) to distinguish that family from others. Even within one family, the crest used in one century may differ from the one used in another.

Mantling

Anyone who's ever climbed into a car in summer knows how hot a metal container can become in direct sunlight. Now imagine wearing a metal bucket on your head. Even in cold climates such as northern Europe, a helmet exposed to the sun quickly becomes suffocating. Fabric coverings were the natural solution, picking up the primary tincture (outside) and primary metal (inside) from the wearer's coat of arms.

Mantling is a curtain of fabric descending from the top of the helm to cover the back and sides. It covers the same area as a shoulder length haircut pulled back. From a wearability standpoint, this is the most practical size, providing maximum shade for the helmet with minimal chance of entanglement.

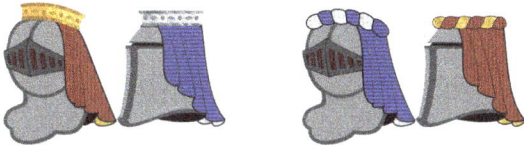

Mantling can be illustrated more expansively, though: a cape billowing as far as waist length, usually in shreds as if ripped during battle. Dangerously impractical on a true battlefield, long capes are used by heraldic artists to fill otherwise empty space around the shield. Alternatively, this same space may be occupied by a robe or collar of office, or that of a knightly order.

Practicality Versus Fantasy

Heraldry is nine centuries old. It did not come into existence fully formed, nor has it remained static. Inspired by the practical and visual reality of medieval weapons of war, heraldry has far outlived its inspiration, freed to wander beyond practicality through pageantry into fantasy. While liberating for the art, this has been problematic for the practice. Heraldry has progressed from:

> the decorating of objects used in actual warfare, through
>
> the decorating of objects used in jousting tournaments, through
>
> the decorating of objects used in solemn ceremonies (funerals, coronations), to
>
> the decorating of objects depicted only in flat art (painted, printed, carved, engraved).

Here's the problem: flat art can depict objects which cannot exist in the real world. Early heraldic artists were witness to knights wielding real weapons and armor as they fought with fellow knights. Artists in later centuries did not have the benefit (or restraint) of seeing how objects were truly supposed to appear. This led to crest designs such as birds in flight unconnected to the torse, ships tossing amid storm-driven waves which somehow neglect to flow off the sides of the torse, and other distractingly nonsensical imagery.

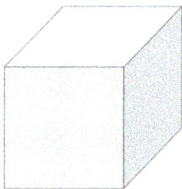

Consider the image at left. It's a cube, yes? Oh, no it isn't. It's a flat square and two flat parallelograms. But it uses the two dimensions of the flat page to suggest a third dimension of depth. Happily, the cube as depicted in 2D can exist in 3D.

Now consider the image at right. With gratitude to M. C. Escher for the original notion, here we have a 2D depiction of an object which cannot exist in 3D. Yes, such a thing could be printed on paper or even engraved shallowly above a torse as a crest. Antiquity argues against it, though, for the simple reason that shields, helms, crests, etc., are meant to be realizable in 3D, even though almost no one actually does this nowadays. If in the future you decide to forge your own suit of armor, how would you craft a crest which would make sense when viewed from all points of view?

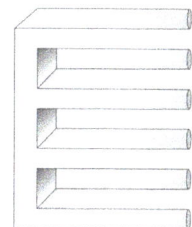

Mottos, Compartments, Supporters

The field and charges within the outline of the shield are all a family needs to express their coat of arms. To also express rank, the appropriate helm or crown or coronet may be added. If the family has a crest, it can be anchored atop the helm. For many renderings of arms, whether printed or painted or carved, this is sufficient. But more embellishments are available, including the lettered name of the family.

Should the shield float in open space, or should it be held up by something? Or rest on something?

Mottos, contrary to popular myth, are not all war cries. In fact, most would be difficult to yell. They tend to be cerebral (Videri Quam Esse, To Seem Rather Than To Be). Many involve a pun on the family's name (Coeur fidele, Heart faithful, for surname Hart). And for some ancient mottos, no one has the slightest idea where they came from or what they mean (Strike, Dakyns, the devil's in the hempe). Mottos are usually depicted written on a ribbon swagging horizontally either above or below the shield. The family name can separately be borne on its own ribbon. The shield can rest on a ribbon placed below it, or hang from one placed above. Names and/or mottos can appear on objects which encircle or otherwise frame the shield.

Compartments, also known as Grounds, are other resting places for shields. They can be literal ground, usually illustrated as a grassy hilltop. They can be architectural, as for example shelving or flooring.

Supporters provide an even firmer grip on the shield. Only rarely granted by nations with a College of Arms, supporters usually come in twos, occasionally human but more often other animals.

Alternatively, arms may be depicted as if set aside after prolonged battle: hung from a tree branch, propped against a spear embedded in the ground, or in some other way artfully arranged.

Badges

Coats of arms are very personal things. They identify the person who heads a family and, by extension, descendants of that person. The family's dinner table may be set with porcelain and silver bearing the coat of arms (or just the crest on smaller items). The coat of arms may be carved in stone above the door, or on fireplace mantelpieces, or wrought into the estate's iron entrance gates.

It is normal for armigerous persons to display their family's coat of arms embroidered in some subtle way on clothing, engraved on a signet ring, flown from a flagpole or even stenciled on a car door.

It is *not* normal for *un*related persons to wear an ally's/employer's full coat of arms. This is where badges come in: they show allegiance to a higher authority without suggesting family relationship.

Powerful people value loyalty and are keen to show loyalty in return (the wise ones, anyway). A knight may bear his own coat of arms, yet in addition bear the badge of his king, making plain whom he would go into harm's way to support. Persons without coats of arms can bear their lord's badge on its own. Wearing a badge says both "I will stand by my lord in battle," and "He will stand by me."

Lancaster	York	Tudor

The most famous use of badges in England came during the War of the Roses, when soldiers on both sides wore a rose as an emblem, the color (red or white) signifying which side they were on. After the war was resolved in 1485, the two colors were merged. Ever since, a combined red and white rose has been the badge of a united England. If this sounds oddly familiar, thank Lewis Carroll for writing *Alice's Adventures in Wonderland* nearly four centuries after the actual war.

The rose never became a charge inside the coats of arms of England or the UK or the monarch. Instead, the rose badge is placed outside the royal shield when depicted in full achievement, growing from a hilly compartment beneath the shield alongside the Scottish thistle and Irish shamrock badges. Since these are not charges inside the royal shield, subjects are welcome to show loyalty by using these badges as charges inside their own arms. But using someone else's shield symbols or badges without welcome is bad form.

Scotland	Ireland

 In UnitedStatesian terms, the eagle-globe-and-anchor symbol of the U.S. Marine Corps is a badge. Whether worn in metal form, or displayed in any other way, that symbol proclaims allegiance and belonging. Marines do not wear the symbols of their commander-in-chief, the U.S. President. But then again, at least as of this printing, no U.S. President has ever earned the right to wear the USMC badge. Respect and loyalty are at their strongest when both flow in both directions in equal measure.

Badges can be created by any family or institution for staff to wear on livery uniforms. For example, the family which owns the green coat below can use its charge as the livery badge for its staff to wear, perhaps as pins or buttons or patches. The blue family which is loyal to the green family is welcome to display the green family's badge outside its own coat, but it would be presumptuous for the blue family to add the green family's internal symbols to the inside of its own coat.

Badges can also arise externally when supporters themselves choose the symbol of their allegiance, in this example a red apple which is not a charge inside the green family's coat. Supporters are welcome to wear the badge they've created on its own, or even incorporate it into their own coats of arms.

Flags–Banners, Pennons, Standards

Flags are pieces of fabric anchored by one edge to a support, the other edges free to catch the wind.

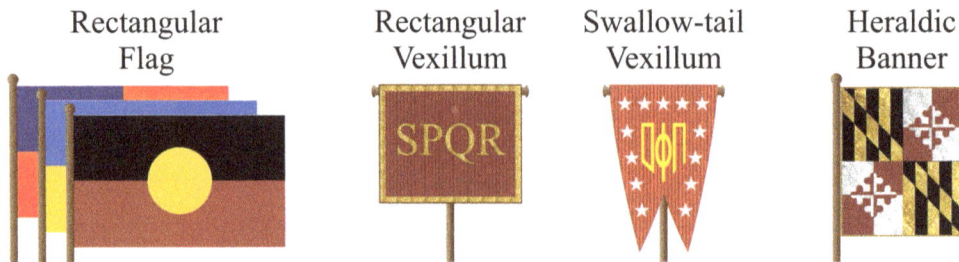

Rectangular Flag	Rectangular Vexillum	Swallow-tail Vexillum	Heraldic Banner

UnitedStatesians often fly the Stars & Stripes flag from their homes to show patriotism. In the heraldic world, though, armigerous persons fly their coats of arms, not for or against patriotism but simply to say, "This is who I am, and I am in this house at this moment." The ruling queen or king of the UK, for example, flies a personal banner which moves from building to building with the monarch. Nobles likewise fly their symbols, not the nation's, above their homes. A popular fad in the US is to fly floral or sport-related flags. Still, why fly someone else's symbols when you can fly your own?

Heraldry provides three broad categories of armorial flag: Banner, Pennon, and Standard.

Banners are the simplest: the coat of arms displayed on a rectangle. The flag of Maryland is the banner of Baron Baltimore in that it contains nothing save the arms of Lord Baltimore, although the flag of Maryland departs from the ideal of a banner in that it is wider than it is tall. Banners are usually either square or slightly taller than wide (noticeably less than 1½ tall by 1 wide). The intent of a banner is to faithfully reproduce a coat of arms on cloth, as undistorted as possible. Since shields are almost always taller than they are wide, fabric of similar proportion serves best.

Coat of Arms **Banner**

Once you have a coat of arms, it's easy to do Pennons. Start with a swallow-tailed vexillum shape, several times taller than wide. Let the background field of the coat of arms fill the whole of the fabric, but don't stretch the charges. Keep them in proper proportion near the edge where the flag will be anchored. Now turn the whole thing sideways, anchor it to a flagpole or spearhead, and carry it proudly into battle.

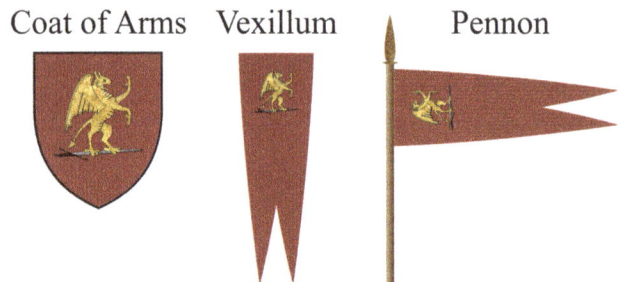

Coat of Arms **Vexillum** **Pennon**

Standards take the concept into overdrive. Like pennons, they're streamers of fabric several times longer than tall. Nearest the hoist, a standard displays the owner's coat of arms in a slightly trapezoidal section. The remainder of the fabric is most often divided per fess (producing an upper and lower half), usually but not necessarily bearing the dominant colors of

Coat of Arms **Badge** **Crest** **Motto** **Standard**

TU ET QUAE LEGIO

the coat. In the foreground, one or more bends (diagonals) bear the motto of the owner's family, while the sections between the bends bear the family's badge and/or crest. The free end of the standard can come to a single rounded point, or twin rounded points (a swallow-tail). Finally, the edging fabric on a standard is typically compony (the two dominant colors of the coat alternating).

Ancestry
Family Surnames

The Western world's current tradition of multi-generational surnames is only about five centuries old. Individuals had given names, of course, but even in a small village there might be more than one John at any moment. To indicate which John they were talking about, other villagers might use:

Father's name: John Robert's son versus John Tom's son

Individual traits: John the graybeard versus little John

Occupation: John the smith versus John the barber

Place: John who lives at the base of the hill versus John who lives by the river

Tribe: John of the Cameron clan versus John of the Bruce clan

Throughout the Middle Ages, these indications were adequate for the vast majority of people. Still, there were shortcomings. If John the smith had a son named George, the son wouldn't be George the smith unless he followed in his father's footsteps and practiced blacksmithing. George would be John's son, but which John are we talking about? He wouldn't be George Robert's son either, because he was Robert's grandson. And solutions like George son of John son of Robert rapidly became cumbersome.

Worse, what if both Johns were graybearded smiths whose fathers were each named Robert? True, that was unlikely in a small village, but economic shifts were about to make it more likely nationwide.

In the 1400s, the Renaissance aided the rise to power of a middle class of society: commoners with uncommon amounts of wealth derived from travel and trade rather than land ownership. In the 1700s, the Industrial Revolution accelerated the migration of villagers to cities: factories were more efficient than cottage crafts, but required large numbers of workers to live close by. As significant wealth began to come from sources other than land, tax authorities began to track individuals as well as fiefdoms. It was during these economic shifts that medieval forms of identification solidified into inherited surnames.

Most people today named Robertson or Thompson or Fernández or MacDonald or O'Connor do not have Robert or Tom or Fernán or Donald or Connor as their father. Lots of people named Underhill do not live under a hill. Just because your surname is Gray, it doesn't mean that you have gray hair (yet). And millions of people named Smith have never forged iron.

More importantly, not all Smiths today are related to one another (being descendants of different smiths). Yes, a search of coats of arms from past centuries will produce at least one armigerous person named Smith. No, this doesn't mean that anyone named Smith today is the direct male descendant of that armiger, nor should modern Smiths adopt that ancient Smith's coat of arms as their own. It is not.

Without confirmation that you are the descendant of a specific armigerous person, it is more honest and self-respecting to adopt a coat of arms of your own devising. Occupational surnames make it easy. So too do many trait names like Gray and Rojas. Don't be afraid to be playful. Since the start of heraldry, armigers have poked fun at their own names, using puns such as a lion for Lyon or León as an easy way to convey the name. Here are just a few to put you in a creative mood:

Gray	Parker	Smith	Cutler	Barber	Molinero	Fletcher	Rojas

It can go the other way, too. Four centuries ago, a German lived in a house which bore a red shield. He called himself "Izaak at the Red Shield." His descendants still use the name Rothschild, but the English pronunciation ("Roth's child") obscures the original meaning (Roth Schild) ("wrote sheet") (Red Shield).

Marshalling–European Style

The founding intent of coats of arms was to identify single individuals during combat. That said, warriors came home, hung their shields on the wall and settled down to married life as landed Gentry. When the eldest son inherited the land, he also inherited his father's weapons. Thus, the shield on the wall gradually came to symbolize the family (the father's eldest son's eldest son's eldest son, anyway).

When the son married a woman whose family was *not* armigerous, the married couple used the only coat of arms available: the son's father's coat. The married couple's coat would in turn descend to the children of the couple.

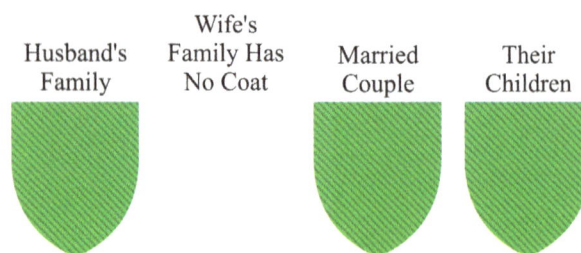

When a son married a woman whose family *was* armigerous, however, things got complicated.

If the woman had *any* brothers, the eldest was the heir to her father's coat of arms. Still, she and her new husband could bear both families' coats of arms on a single shield, divided half and half vertically. Her family's coat would fill the right half of the impaled shield. Her husband's, the left. The children of this couple, however, would not inherit the right to bear their mother's father's coat of arms. That inheritance went to their eldest uncle on their mother's side of the family.

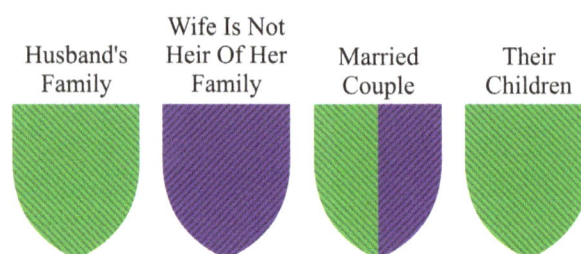

If the woman had *no* brothers, and if she were the eldest sister, then she was the heir to her father's coat of arms. She and her husband could combine the two onto a single shield by placing her father's entire shield, shrunk to roughly one third size, in front of her husband's shield as an Escutcheon of Pretence. This means that her husband held the title

	Wife's Family Has No Coat	Married Couple	Their Children
Husband's Family			

	Wife Is Not Heir Of Her Family	Married Couple	Their Children
Husband's Family			

	Wife Is Heir Of Her Family	Married Couple	Their Children
Husband's Family			

to *her* father's coat of arms during their marriage. Because she was the heir to her father's coat of arms, her children would also inherit her father's arms along with her husband's. The usual way of depicting the inheritance of two coats of arms is quarterly division, with the father's father's coat in the upper left and lower right, and the mother's father's coat in the other two quarters.

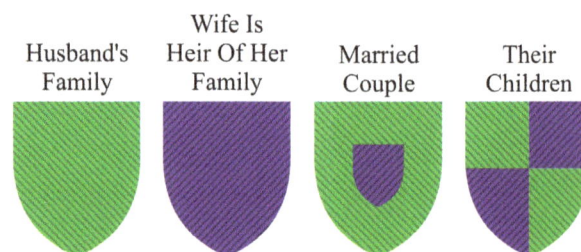

If that couple's eldest son grows up to marry another armiger's daughter, the next generation displays three coats: father's father's father's in upper left and lower right, father's mother's father's in upper right, and mother's father's in lower left. The generation beyond that would display four coats.

Each generation's heir has the choice to marshal all available coats onto one shield, or to pick and choose, or to use just the male line single coat. During the late 1900s, one woman in Europe was heir to over a hundred coats of arms. While it might be fun to see whether an artist could marshal such a vast collection of detail onto one shield, it was more practical for her to use only the most prestigious coats.

The above is the primogeniture tradition (firstborn-male-centric) which has been the standard in Europe for centuries. In countries like England and Scotland where tradition is institutionalized in Colleges of Arms, change comes only after careful forethought. In countries like the U.S. where there is no standards board for heraldry, couples are free to combine their families' coats of arms in any way they choose. All the same, the nearer one stays to tradition, the more dignified the result will appear.

Family Trees

Two patterns for naming dominate modern Western culture:

Single: given name   optional middle name(s)   father's surname

Dual: given name   optional middle name(s)   father's surname   mother's surname

As an example of the single pattern, when Elsa Schmidt married Edmund Garrett, Elsa's father's name was dropped. She became Elsa Garrett, or even Mrs. Edmund Garrett. Aside from being biased against the equality of women, the single pattern also makes it difficult to trace ancestors prior to the mid-1800s. Unless Elsa convinced her husband to give one of their children the middle name Schmidt, a search by her remote descendants may dead-end at Elsa [...?], wife of Edmund Garrett.

As an example of the dual pattern, when Alberto Fuentes married Isabella Verdi, Isabella's father's name was not dropped. Her children's surname became Fuentes Verdi. Only after her son Juan married Sybil Garrett was Verdi dropped. The children of the next generation had the surname Fuentes Garrett. Because mothers' names do eventually drop, the dual pattern doesn't completely preserve all ancestry.

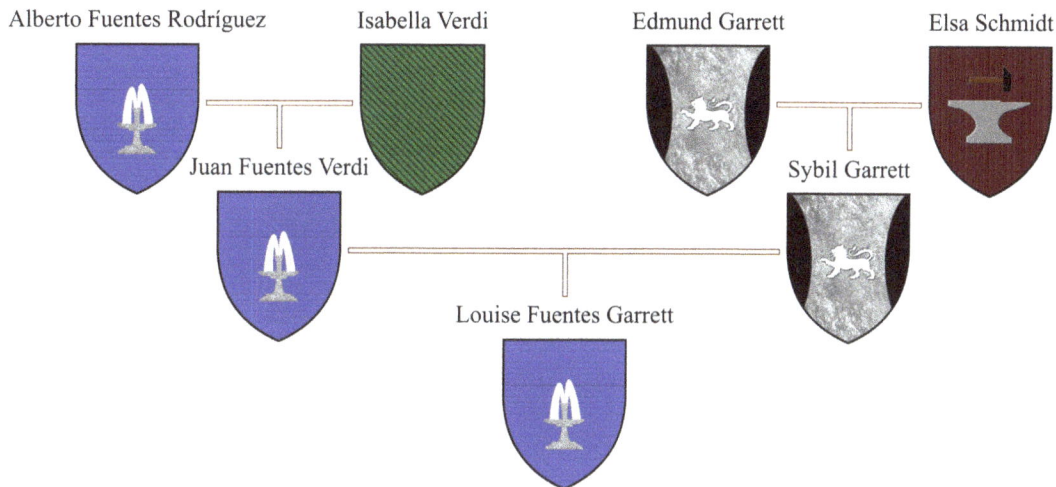

Alberto Fuentes Rodríguez   Isabella Verdi   Edmund Garrett   Elsa Schmidt

Juan Fuentes Verdi   Sybil Garrett

Louise Fuentes Garrett

Marshalling–US Style

The absence of a College of Arms in the U.S. allows for the marshalling of coats in a way not based on primogeniture. Most of us are alive today courtesy of four grandparents, each of whom in turn had four grandparents. Square arrangements (four, sixteen, sixty-four, etc.) equally emphasize each person in every grandparent generation before you.

Fuentes   Garrett

Verdi   Schmidt

Louise Fuentes   Repeating Pattern

FF	MF
FM	MM

Marshalling can be rendered using a full shield shape for each coat (as shown at left) or within quarterly divisions of a single shield shape (as shown at right). To retain some resemblance to European marshalling, let the upper left hand coat of arms be the male line (father's father's father's father, et cetera), but let the *lower right* hand be the female line (mother's mother's mother's mother, etc.). Put another way, the upper left hand follows the Y chromosome, while the lower right hand follows the mitochondrion.

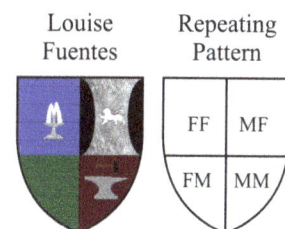

If you trace back far enough, you will not be able to fill in every blank. No one can, not even kings and queens, because eventually we reach a past generation in which no record survives (or was ever created) for the family name of one or both parents. Perhaps a record might be found for Edmund Garrett listing both his parents' full names, yet no record can be found for one of his grandparents.

Place Names and Heraldry

Hereditary Gentry are traditionally identified by the lands they hold: Sir John of Ordsall, Sir Guy of Gisbourne, Le Comte de Monte-Cristo, Manfred Albrecht Freiherr von Richthofen, etc.

Surnames of the Place type were also used by Commoners when far from their birth homes.

In countries whose languages evolved from Roman Latin (Portugal, Spain, France, Italy, Romania, et alia), place names usually began with some variant of de (from), as in Leonardo da Vinci.

In countries whose languages are Germanic (Netherlands, Denmark, Norway, Sweden, Germany, and others), place names usually began with some variant of von or van (from), as in Vincent van Gogh.

Simply stating that one is *from* somewhere doesn't confirm that one governs that place, however. In Germanic countries, to say von und zu ("fon oont tsoo") is to confirm that one is both from a place and is its noble lord. But, depending on the whims of a later monarch, from and to might not forever remain together. For example, eight centuries ago, a Count was assigned to hold the lands of Zinzendorf, thus acquiring the surname von und zu Zinzendorf. Several centuries later, another family was assigned to hold those lands. Since then, the Count's descendants have been von Zinzendorf, but not zu Zinzendorf.

Royal and noble families often have a surname distinct from the place name of their domains. The sovereign nation of Monaco, for example, is ruled by the Grimaldi family. And, for the past century, the family name of the UK monarch has been Windsor.

UnitedStatesians can adopt a similar practice. Say that the Esteban family moved to California four generations ago from Maravatío, Mexico. The family has no ancient arms of its own, and the surname Esteban ("Steven") is of little help in envisioning a new design, so instead they use the civil coat of arms of their home town, identifying themselves heraldically as la Familia Esteban de Maravatío.

Tribal Identity

If your ancestry includes Scots, you may be entitled to wear the tartan pattern of a Highland Clan. There are several dozen major clans, and well over a hundred septs (subsets or affiliates to a clan), each with its proper fabric pattern. Unlike heraldry, tartan is entirely group-focused. Tartans are not created for individuals but rather for extended families. Not every modern person with the surname Cameron will share one specific ancestor named Cameron, but they will most likely have separate ancestors who lived as close neighbors within Cameron lands somewhere in Scotland.

If your ancestry does not include Scots, it is still possible to craft a tartan for your own extended family. Take care, though, to avoid close resemblance to an existing tartan. Many UnitedStatesians have a fascination for tartan but dislike the tartan they are naturally heir to. Unwisely, many of them then choose to wear someone else's tartan because it better suits their taste or palette. They then run the risk of meeting a person who recognizes the tartan, someone who will wonder why the wearers aren't who the tartan says they are. As with coats of arms, it's best to claim only what's yours.

This admonition applies even more strongly against adopting other symbols of tribal identity unless you are a blood descendant of a tribe, or have been brought into that tribe by marriage or adoption.

| Scottish Clan Cameron | Cherokee Nation | Iroquois Confederation | Polish Clan Jastrzębiec |

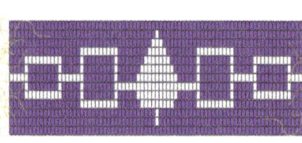

Differences for Cadency

For well over a thousand years, the tradition for inheritance among European noble families has been primogeniture: the eldest son inherits everything. Second and subsequent sons are spares, not heirs. They inherit only if the eldest son dies without producing his own son. Otherwise, their best option is a military career, aiming to earn the king's gratitude and thus be granted their own lands and titles. England's sons have the right to bear their father's coat of arms superimposed with a mark of Cadency.

| Eldest | 2nd | 3rd | 4th | 5th | 6th | 7th | 8th | 9th |

The eldest son's mark is a label: a horizontal line with three or four or five shorter vertical lines hanging from it, centered over the chief (top) of the father's coat of arms. When the father dies, the eldest son removes the label because the eldest son has inherited his father's undifferentiated coat of arms. Second and subsequent sons have their own mark of Cadency, and do not remove it upon their father's death. Only if the eldest brother dies without a son would the second brother inherit the father's coat of arms. Heirs of second and subsequent sons do, however, inherit their own father's Cadency.

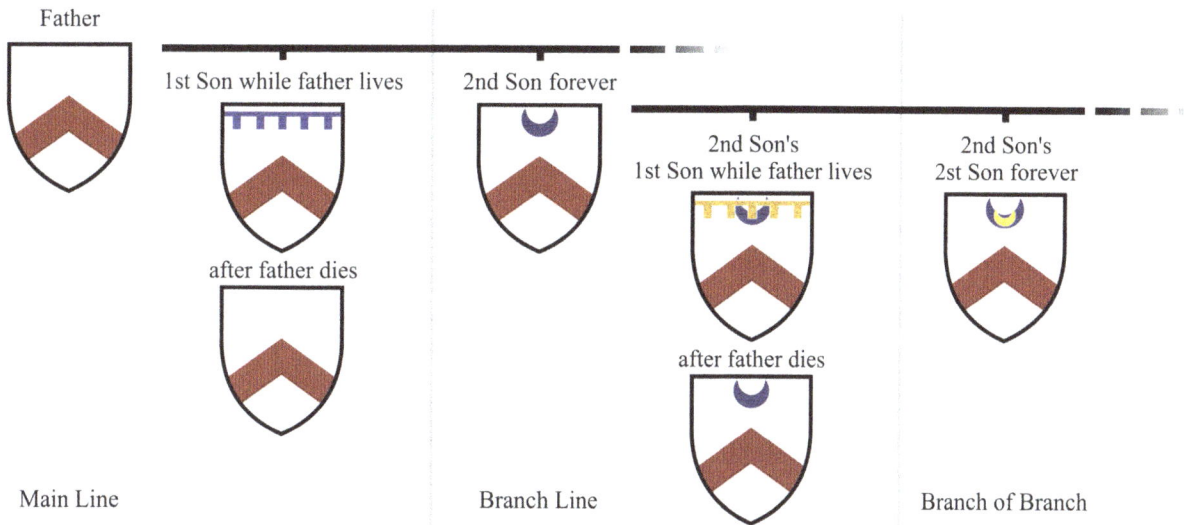

Father

1st Son while father lives

after father dies

Main Line

2nd Son forever

2nd Son's 1st Son while father lives

after father dies

Branch Line

2nd Son's 2st Son forever

Branch of Branch

While it is possible to stack Cadency marks (Branch of Branch), practicality intervenes. Long before a second son's seventh son's fourth son arrives, one of those intervening sons will have acquired a marshaled coat, or been granted new arms, or chosen to forget that he was ever Gentry. That was the way of it with many branch lines who remained in the Thirteen Colonies after they became the United States.

Daughters traditionally were left out of Cadency. In countries such as England and Scotland, this tradition is gradually giving way, as witnessed by the recent decision that the heir to the throne ought to be the eldest *child*, not the eldest son. In countries such as Ireland and the U.S. where rules are not so entailed, there is no reason to limit cadency marks to sons. The firstborn child, son or daughter, can claim the label. Secondborn, male or female, the crescent, etc. Heraldry's enduring influence is due to its traditions having changed as little as possible down through the centuries. Still, they do change when enlightenment insists.

| Radcliffe of Ordsall | Radcliffe of Chadderton | Radcliffe of Todmorden | Worthington of Worthington | Worthington of Blainscough | Steele of Tazewell | Queen or King of the UK | Prince of Wales |

Genealogy

The art of heraldry is an excellent companion to the science of genealogy. Thanks to primogeniture, people with even a little European ancestry are surprisingly likely to have armigerous forebears. Second sons who couldn't inherit European land often sailed across the sea for opportunities. Just twenty generations ago, circa William Shakespeare, possibly a million individuals contributed their genes to your eventual arrival. The Bard himself might not be one of your ancestors, but you could well be the descendant of a knight.

The rise of genealogical databases over the past few decades has brought together billions of facts previously isolated from one another as scribbled notes scattered across six continents. Add to this the growth in DNA databases and it's increasingly possible to reconnect previously lost lines of ancestry.

Legacy

Regardless of which lands our ancestors came from, every one of us is the descendant of people who managed to stay alive long enough to bear children and keep families going from one generation to the next. Heraldry is no longer limited to knights and nobles and royals. We can use this ancient science and art to express who we are by creating new symbols, and to acknowledge our forebears by using their old symbols (even the ancestors who didn't always make the most noble choice). After all, without every single one of them, we would not be here today.

Discussion Questions

1. Next time you're on the road, notice vehicle license plates. What pairs of colors do they use? Where else can you find intentional strong contrast between foreground symbols and background fields?

2. Symbols send messages ("Do not argue with me") ("I'm harmless, mostly)" ("I like the color green"). What messages do you want to send? What charges plus backgrounds might deliver those messages?

3. What is your motto? I like, "YO NO LO HICE" ("*yo* no low *ee*thay") (Spanish for "*I* didn't do it").

4. Speaking of Spanish, why would James *Fox* Meadow sign his name with the initial Z?

5. What does the motto "TU ET QUAE LEGIO?" mean? (hint: Latin didn't have an exact word for army)

6. On the Shield Shapes page, who was Jeanne d'Arc? What can you find out about her?

7. On the Shield Shapes page, where is the Kingdom of Lesotho? What can you find out about it?

8. Who are the Nations of the Iroquois Confederation, and how did their example of wise government guide the much younger United States to separate powers within the U.S. Constitution?

9. Why does the crown of France's heir to the throne have arches in the shape of dolphin?

10. Why do ancient *English* noble names begin with de? (hint: what language did Normans speak?)

11. On the Initials, Ciphers, Monograms page, notice that the book printed in Paris expressed its print date in Roman numerals as MDCCXIX. What year is that in Arabic numerals (our 0 through 9)?

12. A book is a snapshot of the year in which it was printed, whether 2022 or 1719. The best an author can do is present facts as they were understood at the time of printing. I love old science books printed shortly *before* a discovery. On the Mottos, Compartments, Supporters page, the heraldic achievement THE CITY OF LONDON FREEMEN'S ORPHAN SCHOOL comes from "In Starry Realms," a 1909 book which tries to explain why the sun is hot. Its author knew part of the answer: things under pressure become hot. But just 113 years ago, nobody had yet grasped that, with a star-sized amount of pressure bearing down from all directions, the hydrogen at the center of a star fuses into helium, releasing vast amounts of heat and light. We look at past authors and wonder why they didn't recognize facts that seem obvious to us... which begs the question, "What facts do *we* not recognize yet, which will seem obvious to our grandchildren's grandchildren?"

13. Speaking of which, every printing of every book contains errors. When you spot one in this book, please let us know. We'll fix it in future printings as quickly as we can.

14. The stars have been our guides as our species has ventured across every land and sea on Earth. Now we're poised to venture across a vaster ocean, with wayfinders like telescopes and spacecraft to help us see beyond the farthest star. On page 22, what can you find out about the symbol inside the shield supported by two engineers in clean-room suits? Notice what they're gently standing on. At sixty thousand years and counting, we're still inventing new ways to say, "*We were here.*"

Bibliography

Boutell, Charles, and John P. Brooke-Little. *Boutell's Heraldry: With 28 Plates in Colour and Numerous Text Figures.* London: F. Warne, 1983. Print.

Child, Heather. *Heraldic Design: A Handbook for Students with a Foreword by A. Colin Cole.* London: Bell, 1965. Print.

Fairbairn, James. *Fairbairn's Crests of the Families of Great Britain.* Charles E. Tuttle Co, 1968. Print.

Fox-Davies, Arthur C. *A Complete Guide to Heraldry.* London: Bracken Books, 1996. Print.

Hieronymussen, Paul, and Christine Crowley. *Orders, Medals and Decorations of Britain and Europe.* London: Blandford, 1967. Print.

Innes, Sir Thomas, KCVO. *The Scottish Tartans with Historical Sketches of the Clans and Families of Scotland.* Illustrated by William Semple. Edinburgh: W. & A.K. Johnston & G.W. Bacon, 1963. Print.

Louda, Jiri, and Michael Maclagan. *Lines of Succession: Heraldry of the Royal Families of Europe.* New York, N.Y: Barnes & Noble, 2002. Print.

Pine, L G. *Heraldry, Ancestry and Titles.* Gramercy, 1965. Print.

Sprague, Elizabeth, and Curtiss Sprague. *How to Design Monograms.* Pelham, N.Y: Bridgman, 1930. Print.

Znamierowski, Alfred. *The World Encyclopedia of Flags: The Definitive Guide to International Flags, Banners, Standards and Ensigns.* London: Hermes House, 2003. Print.

About the Author

Marc Fountain has been a member of the Society of Children's Book Writers and Illustrators (scbwi.org) since 2016, and a member of the organization for crime writers SistersInCrime.org since 2015, during which time he served for two years as co-President of SinC's North Carolina Triad chapter. A career technical writer nearing 5000 pages of printed and online documentation across dozens of industries, he is also a full-stack programmer with an MBA who begins each contract interview by asking the interviewer what the business objective is.

So why did he write an introductory book about heraldry? "Not quite half a century ago, at age 11, I found a book in my grandfather's library about coats of arms. I was enchanted, but trying to learn from its dense text and colorless line art felt like trying to swim through peanut butter. That book had been written for scholarly researchers the age of my grandfather at the time (my age now). Day jobs and other obligations had to come first, but I've finally gotten round to creating the book I wish had been there all those years ago. If you today are the age I was then, you probably won't notice this paragraph for decades to come. But that was my hope: that different parts of this book would be useful to you at different ages."

Be sure to visit http://CoatsOfArms.ActionableHope.com

Index

Videri Quam Esse

Twine

Ovéquiz

Tu Et Quae Legio

Godfrey

Perdiu En Vuelu

Burke

Diobarach

Nibbs

Solum Duorum

www.ingramcontent.com/pod-product-compliance
Lightning Source LLC
Chambersburg PA
CBHW061223270326
41927CB00024B/3482